A Book of Blessings

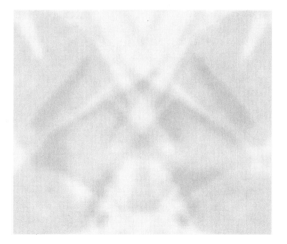

A Book of Blessings

and how to write your own

Ruth Burgess

WILD GOOSE PUBLICATIONS

CONTENTS

LIST OF BLESSINGS

For Cecily, Maggie and Peggy
who have blessed me with
wisdom and love

INTRODUCTION

The Oxford Paperback Dictionary defines BLESS as:

Verb: 1. make sacred or holy with the sign of the cross
        2. call holy, praise; *to bless God*
        3. call God's favour upon; *Christ blessed the children.*

And BLESSING as:

Noun: 1. God's favour; a prayer for this
        2. a short prayer of thanks to God before or after a meal
        3. something one is glad of; *a blessing in disguise.*

Prayers and actions of blessing are found in many cultures and religions. They often accompany 'rites of passage', both secular and religious.

Christianity has inherited from Judaism a rich range of blessings: solemn prayers for an heir[1], psalms of praise to God[2], blessings of crops and flocks[3], festival blessings[4] and the so called Aaronic blessing[5]. There is a tradition that those who pray prayers of blessing for others will be blessed themselves.[6]

Within Jewish writings are a collection of blessings, *b'rakhot*, which relate both to everyday life and to synagogue services and festivals. These include blessings for eating and drinking, the sensual enjoyment of creation, lighting festival candles and recovering from illness. Jewish prayers of blessing always precede rather than follow an action.

Christian tradition includes the blessing of food and the blessing of living creatures and growing things. Manufactured objects can also be blessed as an aid to praise and prayer, as can works of art and natural resources, as evidenced in the use of candles, icons and water in worship. Blessings are also used for important moments in the lives of individuals, for example in baptism and marriage, as well as for the festivals of the Christian year – Advent, Easter, Harvest, etc.

Many prayers from Celtic sources, old and new, include words of blessing. These are prayers that proclaim the goodness of all creation and, as in Jewish sources, acknowledge God's presence in all the moments of our daily lives. Many Celtic blessings are Trinitarian in form and often include references to saints and angels. Whilst older prayers reflect a rural lifestyle, more recent prayers draw their imagery from both urban and rural life.

Blessings can involve more than words. Within many cultures and traditions incense, smoke and water accompany words of blessing, evoking experiences of cleansing and dedication. Within the Christian tradition a spoken blessing is often accompanied by the sign of a cross. The blessing of individuals, particularly children, can include hands being laid on heads. The person giving a formal blessing within a Jewish tradition might wear a prayer shawl. It is easy to visualise Celtic blessings that image the body (*from the crown of my head to the soles of my feet*[7]), incorporating actions to accompany the words. Silence and music, also, can be ways of expressing and accompanying blessings. Sometimes the element of surprise occurs within the experience of blessing.[8] Humour, too, often plays its part.[9]

Many blessings are associated with journeys, both inner and outer, and with places that have long been used for meditation and prayer. There is something about a pilgrimage, with its leaving behind of normal routine, that creates an expectation of blessing and change.

Within different Christian traditions there are issues around the use of 'you' and 'we' in prayers of blessing, and the appropriateness of ordained and lay people using blessing prayers. Some Christians feel that the use of the word 'may' at the start of a prayer of blessing turns it into a prayer of intercession. For others blessing, praise and intercession freely mingle and interchange.

Within this collection of blessings it is often possible to change a prayer for an individual into a prayer for a group of people by changing the word 'you' into 'us', and vice versa. Some blessings are responsive, involving either two voices or two groups of voices, or a worship leader and a congregation. Parts of responsive prayers for all to join in are printed in bold type. The use of an *Amen* at the end of a blessing enables the person who is being prayed for to give their assent to the prayer. However in most cases I have omitted the *Amen*, leaving it up to the reader to decide whether or not to include one. There are no musical settings included in this collection but there is information relating to musical settings of blessings on page 169.

This book also contains some ideas and resources for writing blessings and some suggestions for those who would like to organise a blessings workshop.

Thanks are due to everyone who contributed to this collection of blessings. Also to Hilary de Birch for typing, and to Sheila Auld, Joanne Woodfield and Bernardette Askins for proof-reading, to Ian Cowie for his encouragement, to Marion McNaughton for access to Jewish resources and to Sandra Kramer and the Wild Goose Publications team for their skills and support.

I have greatly enjoyed compiling and editing this book. I hope it will be a useful prayer and worship resource and an encouragement to readers to create blessings of their own.

REFERENCES

1 Genesis 27 v 27f

2 Psalm 103

3 Deuteronomy 7 v 13

4 Deuteronomy 16 v 15

5 Numbers 6 v 24ff

6 Numbers 6 v 27

7 Carmichael, A.,*Carmina Gadelica.* Floris Books 1992. Sleep Blessing, No. 26

8 Matthew 25 v 34ff

9 Genesis 21 v 6

Little Blessings

The keeping of Christ

I set the keeping of Christ about you;
I send the guarding of God with you
to possess you, to protect you,
to accompany you
on all your paths,
through trouble, through danger, through loss.
And I set the dancing of the Spirit around you
to comfort and gladden and inspire you,
each day, each night,
each night, each day.

Kate McIlhagga

A blessing for ditherers

May God the creator
design your life.
May Jesus the teacher
guide your way.
May the Holy Spirit breathe on you
and make you get on with it,
today and every day.

Blessings Workshop, Durham

WALK WELL

Walk well your journey
in peace and in justice.
May you be wrapped
in the shawl of God's loving.
May you be cherished.
May you be blessed.

Ruth Burgess

THE BREATH OF GOD IN YOU

May the breath of God be in you.
May the fire of love we knew from the start
and the peace of the one who makes you new
bring great joy to the cockles of your heart.

da Noust

BLESSING OF LOAVES

Blessing of loaves, blessing of fish,
thousands are fed: a gift of God.
King of that feast, lord of this fare,
bless all we have, bless all we share.

da Noust

Self-dedication

God, bless this trembling offering of myself.

Make me your instrument,
your lute,
carved out, made ready,
silent,
my body the beam,
my desires the strings,
held close to you,
in tune with your heart of love.

God, play your songs through me.

Angela Ashwin

My next-door neighbour

God,
bless my
next-door neighbour
for sometimes
I certainly can't.

Peter Millar

All of creation

Bless to us
loving God
the planet that we live on
and all of creation.

The plants that surround us:
palm trees
sunflowers
poppies and
venus fly-traps.

The animals that are among us:
snails
worms
doves
elephants and
aardvarks.

Bless to us
loving God
the planet that we live on
and all of creation.

Jenni Sophia Fuchs and the children of St Columba's
by the Castle Junior Church, Edinburgh

A MAKING BLESSING

The blessing of God:
Star maker,
Friend maker,
Wisdom maker,
make and remake you
in the image of God.

Ruth Burgess

OUR MAKER, OUR MOTHER, OUR FRIEND

May God our maker, our mother, our friend
wrap us in wholeness
keep us in kindness
and bless our journey homewards.

Frances Copsey

CHANGE

May God bless you:
the Creator working constantly through change,
the Christ who came to share and change our lives,
the Spirit moving in the world and changing it.
May God bless you,
here and now, and for all eternity.

Jan Sutch Pickard

Nights and Days

Sun and Moon Blessing

May the warmth of the sun
shine on you each day.
May the light of the moon
caress you each night.
May the arms of God
enfold you always.
To keep you from fear,
to guard you from harm,
to bless you with love,
to hold you in peace.

Blessings Workshop

Blessings of a New Day

Bless the Lord, O my soul. Bless God's holy name,
who raises us each morning to a new day
bestowing on us its freshness, its promise,
that we may not be captive to the past
but walk in the assurance of forgiveness, which proves
as dependable as is day succeeding day.

Bless the Lord, O my soul, and forget not all his benefits:
wood from Norway which made the bed
wool from Australia which made the coverings
Egyptian cotton for the sheets
a bedside lamp from China –
a world of people committed to give us warmth and safety
till the dawning of the next day.

Bless the Lord, O my soul, who redeems our life from destruction:
so that should terror strike in the night
through human hand or bodily failure
we are kept safe beyond safety, protected beyond all defence,
by Jesus who went before us and endured to the end
who, having won the crown of life, stays at our side
and, if we die, has prepared a place for us.

O my God, how can we give you the praise that is your due?
We wake to you, we sleep to you;
if we take the wings of the morning or let darkness steal over us
to you light and dark are one;
you see us, you shower on us your loving kindness,
you give us life
none shall pluck us from your hand. Blessed be your holy name for ever.

Ian M. Fraser

THIS BLESSED MORNING

God, I feel I could wear the day
I feel I could wear the day today

like a scarf
(But not because it's cold
'cause it's not)

I feel I could wear the day and
the wind would wrap it around and around me

I feel I could wear the day
I feel I could wear the day today
Like a scarf
and dance it

Yellow with a fringe or two of blue

Neil Paynter

LET THE FIRE DIE DOWN

Now let the fire die down,
let the anvil be silent.
Let the peace of God descend this night;
to stay with us,
to comfort and refresh us,
to bless us now and always.

Andrew Foster

A blessing for bath-time at the end of the day

Gracious God, bless this weary body that now craves rest and relaxation;
Lord Jesus Christ, bless this racing mind that seeks peace
    at the end of another demanding day;
Loving Spirit, bless this anxious soul that longs for release
    from shame and regret.

May the warmth of the water enfold me like God's loving arms;
May the smell of the foam carry me beyond the horizon of today's labours;
May the cleansing touch of the soap prepare me for the promise
    and challenge of tomorrow.

Norman Shanks

ALL THROUGH THE NIGHT
a blessing based on Psalm 63

O God, you are my God
for you I long,
like dry waterless lands
so my soul thirsts for you;
your love better than life.
On you I gaze
to see power and glory,
on my lips your praise.

Glory, blessing,
even in darkness.
All through the night,
held by your hand,
yearning for you.

da Noust

Night blessing

May you be out of your depth –
as the deeps of the night sky
contain but cannot explain God's mystery.
May you lose count –
as an infinity of stars
is dazed and amazed by God's presence.
May you be in the dark –
as the moon is eclipsed, but held safe,
with all that is, in the palm of God's hand.
May you be lost for words –
as the Word is spoken
in the silence of the night,
in the beauty of God's creation.

Jan Sutch Pickard

Seasons and Festivals
- a host of dancing things

At the turn of the year

The blessing of God the Creator,
there from the beginning;
the blessing of Christ our Saviour,
God-with-us in history and humanity;
the blessing of the Holy Spirit,
calling us into a future of hope:
be with each one of us,
our communities,
our world,
now and evermore.

Jan Sutch Pickard

Candlemas blessing

Starmaker God,
Lightener of the world;
bless us and warm us
into life and loving.
Bring us to the light of Jesus
all the length and breadth
of our nights and days.

Ruth Burgess

SPRING BLESSING

God bless to us each sign of spring,
each new green shoot,
each lighter day,
each warmer wind.
God bless to us
rebirth.

Kate McIlhagga

EASTER BLESSING

Risen Lord,
give us a heart for the simple things:
love, laughter, bread and wine and dreams.
Give us a green growing hope,
and make of us a people
whose song is alleluia,
whose name is love,
whose sign is peace.

da Noust

A HOST OF DANCING THINGS

Lord God we bless you whose spirit begets a host of dancing things
of insects in the sun
of children at play
of the eyes of lovers in their meeting,
of waterfalls and wind-relishing trees,
of the ballet on stage and on the football field.
We bless you for your delight in your world
and in all living things which inhabit it –
which teaches us to delight in it too
and to join the dancing in heaven
which draws the earth
into a rhapsody of response:
producing a sharing of joy
which presages the Kingdom.

We bless you who meet us, affirm and renew us
at every point of life, in pain as in pleasure.
You have called us by name, and made us your own
so that passing through the waters of grief and suffering
we find you at our side,
no distant God, but one who is afflicted in our affliction,
whose presence with us saves us.

We bless you, our God, who never leaves us nor forsakes us.
We lift up the praise of the whole creation to you,
who are shown, in the life of Jesus Christ,
to be sharer of our joys, a very present help in trouble.
Blessing and honour and glory and power
be ascribed to you, their source, for ever and ever. Amen.

Ian M. Fraser

SUNLIT DANDELIONS

God bless to you
the light and joy
of sunlit dandelions
that know their time
beautifully well
and are perfectly at home
in their own place.

Joy Mead

Dartmoor blessing

In God's name and strength may we be
firm in faith as the granite of the tor,
abundant in caring as the rain on the hills,
warm in loving as the sun on the moor,
joyful in song as the skylark on the wing,
a guide to the path of peace as the stone cross
marks the way. Amen.

St Michael's (Princetown) Trust

*Many stone crosses stand on Dartmoor: most were erected to mark paths across
the moor, some to mark boundaries, and others to mark special places or occasions.*

Little, big moments blessing

May you stop and see
the way light falls and rocks glow,
and may God bless you with
little, big moments that make your heart dance.
Moments when you suddenly become aware of all the
overwhelming beauty and wonder and richness and love
living in the middle of where you are standing already.
Moments when you gaze around understanding:
the kingdom of God is now.

Neil Paynter

GOD OF THE HARVEST

God of the harvest
who has given us so much;
help us to be generous like you,
that the world may know your goodness and blessing.

Simon Taylor

THE BLESSING OF AUTUMN

As Autumn flames across park and field
as smoke curls from ditch and garden
as birds sing their farewell song
as frost begins to touch the ground
and our hearts are warmed
by the scent, sound and touch of it,
then is the time to throw away
the heavy stones of anger, regret and fear,
which harden our hearts.
Now is the time to gather stones of praise
to build a cairn of thankfulness to our God
for all the blessings of our Autumn life.

Kate McIlhagga

THE TRUE SPIRIT OF CHRISTMAS

May the true spirit of Christmas
be with us all this Christmastide:
the spirit of joy that overflows from the heart
and makes neighbours rejoice,
the spirit of peace that harmonises differences
and makes music of our common life,
the spirit of love that sings the mind
of God to the world.
May the true spirit of Christmas
be with us all this Christmastide,
and for ever.

Jack Kellet

CHRISTMAS

The blessing of the manger –
God's creation all around;
the blessing of the shepherds –
God's people with feet on the ground;
the blessing of the angels –
good news for all, and peace for the world,
be with you
now and for ever.

Jan Sutch Pickard

Do not be afraid

Do not be afraid –
white wings soar over the Machair
and skim the waves.

Do not be afraid –
children with tinsel haloes sing
old words, with new wonder.

Do not be afraid –
bright constellations dance
in the winter sky.

Do not be afraid –
the air trembles with God's presence
where we pray.

Do not be afraid –
be ardent and amazed;
active, passionately, for peace,
alive to God's glory in the here and now,
aware of angels everywhere.

                                    Jan Sutch Pickard

At the ending of a year (or other ending)

Bless this threshold Lord
sweep it clean with blessing

Bless my vision Lord
give me eyes for seeing

Bless my footsteps Lord
shoe me well with meaning

Bless my pathway Lord
lead me in your teaching

Bless all pilgrims Lord
give them hearts for tending

Bless our pilgrim world
home to you amending.

Yvonne Morland

Moments of Our Days

HERE AND NOW

For the unexpected wonder
of love and life and laughter
bursting through my world
like an explosion of stars;

for the wonder of my person
for the people and the journey
which have brought me to this place,
here, now;

for hope, and wonder and awe
at the future:
at all the adventures
the years may contain;

for all these things
I am so richly blessed;
I am brim full of the wonder
of God bedding down in me.

Rosie Miles

BIRTH BLESSING

As I cup my hand
around your head
little one
may God hold you
and keep you.

As I rock you
in my arms
little one
may Christ shield you
and encompass you.

As I bend to kiss your cheek
little one
may the Spirit bless you
and encourage you.

Kate McIlhagga

Blessing for a placenta

This ceremony involves burying the placenta and planting a tree over it. It should be carried out in the presence of the baby and parent/s, possibly by the parent/s.

God our creator and nurturer,
as the earth receives this placenta
let us give thanks for the way it sustained the life of N… in N…'s womb.

The blood on our hands carries life, pain, birth.
May it now nourish this tree with its vitality.

May the mingling of blood and soil
remind us of our constant connectedness to the earth.

As we see the tree grow
may we be blessed with the joy of life and respect for your creation
and be earthed in the reality of your love.
Amen.

    Zam Walker Coleman

A blessing that could be used after a miscarriage or abortion

Place a symbol for the baby and light a candle.

Compassionate God,
I ask you to bless my baby
and surround her/him with your love.

I ask you to bless me
in my time of loss, grief and continuing bereavement.

I ask that you sustain me
as my body readjusts,
that you uphold me
as I encounter pity and judgement,
that you enfold me
as I come to face the difficult questions in myself and others.

Give me the courage to embrace the pain,
the pain of the end of this possibility,
in order that I may move forward
in truth and love and hope.
Amen.

    Zam Walker Coleman

A WELCOME BLESSING
(for Lorna)

Welcome Lorna.
You arrived with the summer roses
petals unfolding, fragile and fragrant,
shaken by the rainstorms,
warmed by the strengthening sun.

Welcome Lorna.
May your life unfold
in warmth and beauty.
May the angels protect you
and the saints tell you stories.
May you be caressed and cherished
and cradled in love.

Welcome Lorna.
May you bring joy
to all who meet you.
May you grow each day
in grace and in wonder.
May you be blessed
with the wildness
and wisdom of God.

                                   Ruth Burgess

BLESSING FOR AN ADOPTIVE FAMILY

Bless the family who adopted my son,
for giving him what I could never have done.
Bless his new mother and father,
his new brother and sister too.
I wish all God's Blessings to follow you.

Linda Fraser

BLESSING AT THE PLACEMENT OF A CHILD FOR ADOPTION

The blessing of God be on this child;
surrendered in love and pain,
received in love and joy.

The blessing of God be on these parents
who brought this child into life,
gifting him/her love and talents.

The blessing of God be on these parents
who receive him/her into their lives,
promising him/her love and nurture.

The blessing of God be on us all,
the blessing of love unending.
The blessing of hope and life.

Pat Welburn

Note: Where appropriate the names of the parents and child can be used.

GROUNDED AND ROOTED IN LOVE

(Julian of Norwich: *The whole of life is grounded and rooted in love …*
… without love we cannot live)

We all know dispossession, God.
Just when we were settling in,
kicked out of the womb without a
by your leave
and having to begin life afresh.

And that was only the first time.
We put down roots, got comfortable,
then puberty!
And the whole wretched business started
again. On your bike.

There's no stopping
where you know where you are,
life's not like that,
growth's not like that.

All the same we're the lucky ones.
Got roofs over our heads, got
more.
Got people who care, friends
who are home for us,
give us root room. It's a blessing.

Make us gardeners
of others, God,
turn the compost
of our tangled intentions, our weak-stemmed loving,
into fertile soil.
Help us nurture others,
ourselves, too.
Ground us and grow us all
into the beauty which is
You.

Frances Copsey

LORD OF ALL LIFE, I BLESS YOU

May the God who knew me be praised!
Who knew me when I was but a speck of life
who knew me as I took shape in the womb
who knew me in childhood and as I grew up
who has known me till this day.
Beyond the perceptions of mother and father
beyond the insights of a life-partner
beyond my own self-understanding.
Such knowledge is too wonderful for me, high, unattainable,
such knowledge is yours, the Lord of all life. I bless you.

Such knowledge is yours, the Lord of all life
and yet you do not reject me or put me to shame.
You cannot be fooled by appearances,
I cannot hide away from your eyes the ways I let you down.
You see with a sharpness which no human eye can match,
and yet you love me
you clothe me with the garment of Christ's life
you see me as I am in him.
Such knowledge is too wonderful for me, high, unattainable
such knowledge is yours, the Lord of all life. I bless you.

I revel in your presence,
I bless you, my heart singing and bursting with joy,
my feet dance and my body sways in delight,
when I realise that your love is not dependent
on my ability to respond worthily: it is there in any case.

Bless you, Lord God; blessed be your holy name for ever;
and let all the people say 'Amen'.

Ian M. Fraser

A WEDDING OR RELATIONSHIP BLESSING

In the starshine and sunshine of God
may you be warmed and welcomed.

In the stories and laughter of Jesus
may you be called and challenged.

In the fire and breath of the Holy Spirit
may you be awakened and kept from harm.

May your home be a place of hospitality and kindness,
a beckoning lamp in the darkness,
a shelter for questions and dreaming,
a safe space for joy and tears.

Live well _____ and _____
May you celebrate life together
May you grow in love for each other
May you dance with the little ones,
the saints and the angels,
May you be cherished
May you be blessed.

Ruth Burgess

Knowing her blessing

Loving Mother,
who with perfect timing
knows when to push; to nudge; to shove;
and when to wait,
even though panting for change.
Grant us the courage to name you;
and the grace of your timing.

Sister Christ,
who feeds us with warm breast milk
when the heavenly feast is too rich a fare;
and in whose death our own wounds find resurrection.
Teach us also to play with you,
that we may know the delight
of your particular freedom.

Lady Wisdom,
who nurtures and wills our growing.
Lead us in your wild dance,
that we may tread the unfamiliar paths
singing gladly;
and find fulfilment for the dreams
that fit your knowing of us.

Chris Polhill

MID-LIFE BLESSING

May the blessing of the Maker be yours,
warmth and welcome and stars dancing in darkness,
circling you, cherishing you.

May the blessing of the Storyteller be yours,
, justice and joy and bread for the journey,
challenging you, inspiring you.

May the blessing of the Holy Spirit be yours,
wind and fire and a bright shawl of wisdom,
disturbing you, comforting you.

May the blessing of friends and strangers be yours
angels and saints and little ones playing
encouraging you, befriending you.

Blessings be yours
in the midst of your journey;
May you be blessed with integrity and courage
in good times and bad times.

May you be strong and happy and creative.
May you be cradled and held in love.

Ruth Burgess

ON RETIREMENT

God bless you
as you embrace the future.
God bless you as you lay down the past.
God bless you in the present moment
with lively hope and hopeful life.

Kate McIlhagga

THE TIME THAT'S LEFT

God bless to me the time that's left:
to hold the child,
to see another spring,
to tidy my room,
to forgive and forget,
to reach out and befriend,
to live my life in peace and joy.
God bless to me
eternity.

Kate McIlhagga

For a friend who is dying

Creator,
Enfolder,
Guide.
From first to last our strength.
You brought us into the world,
walk with us now we pray.
Guide us.
Encourage us.
Comfort us.
Then, when the tide turns,
and we are ready to go,
bring us safely ashore,
into your welcoming embrace.

Jean Murdoch

Blessing at a time of death

Ground of our being, gift of our longing,
in sadness we come to you, aching in our hearts,
and yet rejoicing in our souls, for this life
well-lived and fully fashioned in its myriad tones.

Yvonne Morland

Go gently on your voyage

Go gently on your voyage, beloved.
Slip away with the ebb tide,
rejoice in a new sunrise.
May the moon make a path across the sea for you,
the Son provide a welcome.
May the earth receive you and the fire cleanse you
as you go from our love
into the presence of Love's completeness.

Kate McIlhagga

Work and Leisure

A BLESSING ON MY LAPTOP

God bless my laptop as I switch it on this morning;
May its memory successfully guard my hard-wrung thoughts;
May its programmes accommodate my lack of know-how;
May its 'help' processes be clear when I get lost;
May its spell-check speak English and not American;
May it be humble enough to let me think I'm still in charge;
May our relationship today be short and satisfactory.

Norman Shanks

BEFORE A MEETING

As our eyes meet
and our hands touch in greeting,
may Christ within each of us bless our meeting.

Be Christ in the space
between hearing and speaking,
opinions that differ,
facts and wishes.

And may Christ redeem every hidden agenda,
that in this place,
at this time,
God's will be done.

Chris Polhill

A blessing for meetings

Living God, bless this gathering –
that through discussing and deciding
your will may be done and your kingdom advanced;
Jesus, our Friend, bless us as we get down to the agenda
– that we may take time and make space to listen to one another;
Reassuring, challenging Spirit, bless our thoughts and our words
– that we may have the insight to see what you are prompting us to say and do,
and the courage to follow it through.

Norman Shanks

At the office door

Lord pour your blessings on all who work here
Inspire our shared efforts
Give proportion to our rivalries and jealousies
Join us together to create your kingdom

Nick Burden

A blessing for working in a shop

May you be treated with value
may your exchanges be friendly
may you have enough change

and at the end of the day
may you find a balance.

Neil Paynter & Helen Lambie

A blessing for a work day

May God bless you
as you manage your work,
as you take painful decisions.
May God bless you
as you relate to others,
and give you strength for the day ahead.

Kate McIlhagga

When you go to work

When you go to work
may God itch your memory
and tickle you into laughter
and bring a friend to throw their arms around you.

Blessings Workshop

A blessing for a computer

God bless this computer:
a heap of switches
that go on and off.
God bless my body:
kilos of chemicals
and a shallow bath of tepid water.
God bless our world:
a minor rock
in major space.
God bless us with wonder.

David Coleman

WISDOM

May God's wisdom guide you
wherever you walk in this world;
may God's wisdom encourage you
in your daily work;
may God's wisdom work in you like yeast
and rise in you like hope!
May you taste and see God's goodness
and may God's wisdom be your delight
now, this night, and for evermore.

                              Jan Sutch Pickard

GOD BLESS DAYS OFF

God bless days off
with no one to call back but
oyster catchers and herring gulls

nothing to pick up but messages left in the landscape

(how sometimes life is like a thousand shades
you could never begin to describe. And
sometimes life is simply blue sky, green grass, white waves)

No one to get in touch with but
myself again

No deliveries to pick up but
what the waves leave at my feet –
(periwinkles, cowry shells, pieces of coloured glass like
precious stones, willow-pattern china)

No details to get lost in but
the business of a rock pool
Nothing to follow up but
the path of a shore-crab

Nothing to file but ideas for poems

Nothing to note but the taste and texture
and salty, sharp smell of the day

God bless days off
and time to retreat into

Time to discover new energy to
take back into work

to serve God more fully

Neil Paynter

PUB BLESSING

Bless this pub
where the snooker table slants with saving grace
where brass is polished with devotion

Where we sit at a table
buying rounds, sharing crisps
getting drunk on lager and conversation and
wine that makes us glad

Where the jukebox plays sacred music –
numbered chants and anthems
we flip through
choosing favourites

Bless this neighbourhood pub –
alight and alive with laughter –
where we confess our failures
celebrate our victories
pray for health and happiness and true love
give thanks for friends
sing
and raise our glasses to
life in all its fullness.

                              Neil Paynter

BLESSING FOR A SABBATICAL
(for Rosie)

May you enter trustingly into this sabbath space
May you enter quietly into this sabbath rest
May you enter joyfully into this sabbath play

Let your body unfold in this sabbath
Let your mind unwind into this sabbath
Let your spirit expand into this sabbath

May it reveal its secrets to you gently
May it embody its truth in you authentically
May it release new life in you abundantly

So go with gladness into this sabbath
Go with gratitude into this sabbath
And may the God who rests on the sabbath
look at her labours in you
and proclaim, 'It is very good.'

Nicola Slee

Houses and Homes
– dwellers and dwellings

FROM A BLESSING OF A CROFT

O God and Father of all creation,
We, your children, seek your blessing on this land entrusted to us.

Lord Jesus, Word of God made flesh,
speak your word of peace to this family,
these buildings, this land.

Spirit of the Living God,
empower us now to convey the blessing of God
to empower your children to live and work
in the light of your love.

We bless this family now:
In the name of God, from whom every family on earth
and in heaven is named,
In the name of Jesus who came for us, died for us, rose for us,
In the name of the Holy Spirit who gives us love, wisdom and strength.
The blessing of the Holy God be upon you.

In the name of the Father, Creator of heaven and earth,
In the name of Jesus who lived in the home of Joseph and Mary,
In the name of the Spirit whose home is in our hearts,
The blessing of God be upon this home, and upon all these buildings.

In the name of the High God, our shelter and our security,
In the name of Jesus our peace,
In the name of the Holy Spirit who guides us,
You holy angels guard the boundaries of this land,
the gates and doors, dykes and fences,
the going out and the coming in.

In the name of God, we bless this garden,
let it bring forth beauty and food for the children of God,
let it be a place where God walks with his beloved.

In the name of God we bless this field and all that lives in it,
to make it fruitful, to the glory of God
and the good of his children.

And now with the host of angels,
and with the great cloud of witnesses unseen
who encompass us,
having reached home before us,
we join in the eternal hymn:
Holy, holy, holy, Lord God of Hosts,
heaven and earth are full of thy glory.
Glory be to thee O Lord most high.

Ian Cowie

Blessing for a home

I've come to know a place I can call home:
It walls me gently round, it gives me space,
It offers me stillness, it contains my fears,
It roofs me safely under, gifts me grace,
It is both books and art, colour and light,
It shelves and stacks me, my life storage space;
It's work and love and dust and green growing things,
It's laughter, friends and food, it's cat's own place,
It is so full of me and all I am,
I've come to know a home, a sacred space.

Rosie Miles

Bless to me my dog

God of all living creatures,
bless to me my dog:
a constant friend,
whose 'I love you'
is wordless
who gives and greets
guides and protects
unconditionally.

Joy Mead

BLESS MY CAT

Bless my cat
for she is the pinnacle of creation:

Bless her wildness and warmth,
Bless her long fur,
Bless her tail of great worth,
Bless her ability to snore;
Bless her considered dedication to *Felix*
Bless her company,
Bless her thunderous purr,
Bless her finding of me;
Bless her utter catness,
Bless her sharpened claw.

Bless, God of felines,
all who travel their way,
night and day,
through the open cat door.

Rosie Miles

BLESS YOU!
(for a new 'Bed and Breakfast' house)

Upon the traveller who has sought refuge here,
the blessing of Him
who had nowhere to lay His head.

Upon the weary and travel-stained,
the blessing of Him
who washed His friends' feet.

Upon the hurt one who has come to find
healing in the beauty of hills and loch,
the blessing of the Good Shepherd.

Upon the lonely one who comes alone,
the blessing of Him who promised to be
with you always.

Upon the worried one who
seeks to get away from it all,
the blessing of the Lord of Peace.

*My peace I give unto you,
let not your heart be troubled or afraid.*

Ian Cowie

A home filled with God
(for Andrew, Amanda, Billy and David)

May God the maker bless you,
may you delight in the sunlight
and starlight and surprises
of the turning earth.

May Jesus the carpenter bless you,
may you celebrate life together
in all its struggles and joy.

May the Holy Spirit bless you,
may you dance with the saints and the angels
in the wisdom and the wildness of her love.

May your house be a shelter of strength and of welcome;
a laughter of music and stories,
a safe space to ask questions,
an engine whistle of exhilaration,
a smooth stone of stillness,
a warm hug in the darkness,
a home filled with God.

Ruth Burgess

Blessing for a Family*

A harlequin stone for the child
from her first nursery picture
to her latest 'creation'.

A mottled stone for the child
straying far at times
in mind or body.

A polished stone for the child
when constant in love
and a faithful friend.

A weathered stone for the child
on whom experience
has left its mark.

A glistening stone for the child
when he loves himself
and himself is loved.

A stone of memory for the child
lent us a while
now gone elsewhere.

Six stones of Grace upon us all.
A cairn to the Trinity

that triune family
of energy, love
and sacred unity.

                    Judith Rack

* Notes:
To be said by mother and/or father after many years as parent(s). May be adapted
as required or desired. Several stones are needed with differing characteristics: as
the blessing proceeds a small pile is built up – the 'cairn' of the last verse.

For the blessing of friends

We are humbled with blessing
dear God, and we bless you,
for the lives you have gifted us
in the shape of our friends.

Such caring, such holding,
such sharing, such scolding,
softening our hardnesses
freeing our pain.

Gladly we lift up
our friends for your blessing
returning them home
to your joy once again.

                    Yvonne Morland

SHARING, LAUGHING AND LISTENING

The blessing of
sharing
laughing
listening

The blessing of
comforting
supporting
shielding

The blessing of
forgiving
trusting
respecting

The blessing of
honouring
cherishing
loving

The blessing of friends.

                    Jenni Sophia Fuchs

Inner Journeys
- going and growing

WHEN YOU SEEK GOD'S HELP
a blessing based on Psalm 34

When you seek God's help
know that your prayers will be answered;
Though you are afraid
trust that you will be set free from fear;
Put yourself in God's hands
and you will taste God's goodness;
Look to the light
and your face will be bright with joy.

Jan Sutch Pickard

A BLESSING ON INNER DARKNESS

Bless to me, O Lord,
the darkness in my journey,
the wounds of deepest longing,
the risk of still believing.

O intimate, incarnate One,
stay close where I most need you,
where you already are:
in my mistakes – healing;
in my emptiness – inflowing;
in my nothingness – God.

Angela Ashwin

BLESSING IN TIMES OF EMPTINESS

For I will lead her out
deep into the desert,
and there I will speak,
speak to her heart.

When Jesus won't be found,
set your face once more;
remembering the feast,
hunt for him there

da Noust

FOR THE GIFTS OF CREATIVITY

Your blessing God, on the gifts of creativity
emerging, stumbling, stretching, growing,
risking all that we have and are
for the joy of possible connection.

And Your blessing God, on the places and people
who know our need for creativity, and nurture
our tentative efforts into full-bodied, undulating,
elongating, syncopating, blooming, blessed beauty.

For the power of these processes
We give you great praise.

Yvonne Morland

LET LIGHT ENFOLD ME

Let light enfold me
that my inward eye may see clearly
the path that lies ahead.
Let my mind be opened up
that I may recognise
the sign posts along the way.

Grant me the wisdom
that comes from understanding
the true from the false.
And guide my steps,
so that should I falter or stumble,
tripped by former beliefs
that blind me still,
I may go forward with courage,
and with the determination
which persistence brings.

Let me be embraced
with the love by which
the whole creation is moved,

the very essence with which
all things are held together,
dependent yet independent,
whole yet individuated,
in which all are my relatives.

Anon

LIGHT AND DARK
A blessing based on Psalm 139

Light and dark are as one to You,
in womb-darkness You formed us.

Bless this inner darkness;
Give courage to embrace it,
Give wisdom to live it,
Soul friends for the journey.

That from this dark also
a birthing may come.

God making us, beside us, within us;
Light and dark are as one to You.

Chris Polhill

FOR TIMES OF DRYNESS

We ask your blessing mother God,
on our times of dryness,
when the well of living water
seeps into barren land.

Help us to be, to listen in the waiting
for the still small voice
which speaks of promises unbroken
beneath our doubt and fear and forgetting.

And when the river returns to us, Creator God
teach us to praise the bounty of water,
to use its succour well, to succour others,
flowing with the love which comes from you.

Yvonne Morland

WRESTLING FOR A BLESSING ...
PRAYERS OF THE NORTHERN SAINTS

Watch, watch
for the bright shining light in the sky.
Aidan and Hilda have passed through
the gate of glory.

Listen, listen
for the sound of prayer

rippling through the waves.
Cuthbert is knocking at heaven's door.

Sing, sing with Caedmon
the song of God's wonders
in sand, sea and stars.

Be aware of the saints
beside and around you:
the keepers of wisdom;
the hospitality givers,
the teachers and healers:
those who shine with the uncreated light of God.

Let all the earth be glad
and the heavens resound
with the delight of God's people.

As Hilda returned to the north
as Columba left Ireland,
not with joy and praise
but with struggle and reluctance;
so let us wrestle for a blessing
walk with a limp
pray with a question
put our hands in the wounds
of your world, elusive God.

Kate McIlhagga

For light and for darkness

Come to us Creator God
so that we may praise you.
Wrest the clutching shadow from us
cast it into cloth for stars.

Bless each time of darkness in us
help us bear it into light.
Turn us round from running forward
still in us desire for flight.

Come to us Creator God
so that we may praise you.
Wrest the clutching shadow from us
cast it into cloth for stars.

Yvonne Morland

When the Road is Hard

SOMETIMES PAIN SWEEPS OVER ME

Lord

Sometimes pain sweeps over me –

pain of limbs, pain of heart.

There is heaviness in movement and thought.

But why am I telling you this?

You already know and are bearing it with me –

Enabling me to carry on –

Blessing me with your strength and love.

Joyce Clarke

BLESSING IN GRIEF AND LOSS

You will know sorrow

But your grief will turn to joy.

And that joy,

No one,

No one will ever,

No one will ever take from you.

da Noust

BLESSING FOR THOSE IN DISTRESS

May you come safely to shore
across the dark ocean

and know
that even in the darkest depths

there is hope to be found
and peace.

          Mary Taylor

IF OUR DAYS DARKEN

If our days darken
May hope bud within as the ivy does,
Blossoming into green, unexpected flowers when the winter comes.

          Frances Copsey

BLESSING FOR THOSE WHO HAVE NO ONE LEFT TO TALK TO

Listening God, bless all those
who have no one left to talk to
who are afraid
friends will reject them,
families will disown them
and lovers will leave.

Bless them with the confidence, loving God,
that no matter what they confess
you love and accept them,
understand their shadow and their light,
will never leave them feeling ashamed, poor, alone.

Neil Paynter

IN TIMES OF AFFLICTION

May we discover that the road we didn't choose
didn't want to travel,
is a highway that leads unerringly
towards the light.

Frances Copsey

I NEED YOU TO BLESS ME

I need you to bless me,
Take my hand;
I need you to bless me,
I listen to the wind;

I'm wrestling with angels,
I'm touching the storm,
My body is broken,
My mind is torn,

So I need you to bless me,
I need it now;
I need you to bless me,
Please don't go.

Rosie Miles

BLESSING FOR THOSE WHO ARE DEPRESSED

God be with all those who are depressed.

Bless them with the support
and understanding
of friends and family,
and be close to those without family or friends.

Protect them, sheltering God,
and help them make their home in you.

Neil Paynter

Turnings, Endings and New Beginnings

TURNINGS

Beauty is amongst us,
turning our sorry heads
when we least expect it.
Hidden in the bare words,
but listened for. Listen.

The crops are in flower,
turning towards the sun,
following all the day.
For them the day's enough,
the time they have's enough.

As if a highwayman
held us up with pistols
to give us all he had
and rode away laughing,
his pouches still full.

On a ghostly stallion
the rider turns from war.
His army turns behind,
to learn what ploughs are for
that ghostly horses draw.

I am turning again
to watch the horizon.
Soon there will be a sail.
There is a boat coming,
always a boat coming.

The reasoning mind waits,
settling between what is
and what it believes in.
Finally accepting.
Now, make a beginning.

Robert Davidson

A BLESSING FOR BEGINNINGS OR ENDINGS

May God who is Alpha and Omega
be present in all our world's endings, endurings and beginnings,
to bless, sustain and renew all creation
and to work the redemption and completion of all time.

Nicola Slee

LEAVING A FAMILIAR PLACE
(savouring the moment)

Lord, bless our leave-taking of a familiar place.

Enable us to gather around us the belongings necessary for our journey,

and then to take pause and consider what this place means to us;

memories silted up in every corner of rooms

whose walls have breathed us in and out over the years.

If our leaving is a good one,

let us carry forward a balance of rich pickings

to finance our future.

If sad,

bless us with the will to examine our bad debts

and learning from them,

cut our losses

and move on.

                    Sylvia Pearson

BLESSING ON LEAVING ABUSE

Use two symbols: one for what you are leaving and
the other for the next stage of your journey.

Resurrection God
I ask your blessing
on this step into the unknown,
on this leap of faith into freedom.

I do not know what awaits
but I know what I am stepping out of:
the chains of fear, contempt, control;
the continuous undermining,
the stifling of life,
the brutal imprisonment of abuse.

I choose to embrace liberation, respect and integrity.
I choose to grow, to thrive, to blossom in new life.
I choose to take the risk of trusting in myself and in you.

Fill me with your grace and enable me
to be fully the person you created me to be.

Zam Walker Coleman

BLESSING FOR A FRIEND GOING ON A LONG JOURNEY

Wherever you walk
May the earth uphold you;
Wherever you enter
May you find welcome;
Wherever you nest
May it be a good home.

And wherever you go
in these great wide worlds
within and without,
know that my thoughts go with you.

Rosie Miles

A FAREWELL BLESSING

As we part, my friend, may the love of God keep you safe in all your journeying;
May the risen Christ guide your feet in the way of justice, joy and hope;
May the Spirit encourage and accompany you wherever you go –
until we meet again.

Norman Shanks

BLESSING ON THE START OF A NEW ENDEAVOUR

Lord,

I am casting off my boat into unfamiliar waters.

I am afraid of storms,

of uncharted seas

and the hostility of other sailors.

Be beside me,

my navigator, my steersman, my guide.

Keep my eyes looking forward,

my ears open to your instructions,

my voice ready to reflect your word.

Jean Williams

FOR A GOODBYE

Blessed the road on which you go today.

There is Jesus, waiting in love.

Go in peace, granted forgiveness,

For he knows you are his friend.

da Noust

Setting Out, Going Forth

Go forth in Faith, Hope and Love

Go forth now,
in the Faith which overcomes the world,
in the Hope which will not disappoint you,
in the Love which never fails.

You are ambassadors of Christ
and He is with you always.

Grace, mercy and peace,
from Father, Son and Holy Spirit,
bless, preserve and protect you all this day
and for ever.

Ian Cowie

The shield and fire of God

As you go from this place
and on to many others,

May the shield of God keep you
from the harm without,

And the fire of God consume
the harm within.

Blessings Workshop

Departure at the end of a women's workshop day

Loving God, bless us
as together we go out,
empowered by our longing,
strengthened by our solidarity,
humbled by our need,
to love and serve the world

                                    Yvonne Morland

Going out

As we go out from this place
may we be
full of desire and wonder,
full of longing and praise
and full of the courage to love.

                                    Rosie Miles

Living letters of his word

May God write his message upon your heart,
bless and direct you,
then send you out
living letters of his word.

                                    Neil Paynter

A Blessing for a visitor to England

May God go with you
as you journey through this land.

May the saints of ancient times
be your guiding lights.

May you find their pathways
a delight to wander and explore.

And may the love of God, in Jesus Christ
grow in you and bless you,
giving you strength and faith.

Blessings Workshop

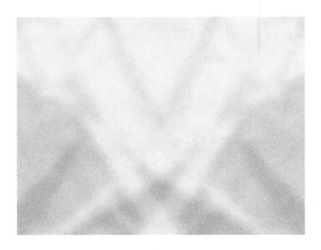

HELEN'S LEAVING PRESENT

A prompted cuddle,
a moment's pause,
and an unsolicited kiss
as only a three-year-old can.

You on your toes,
me on my knees,
equal in loving.

This was my journey blessing,
and nothing
could have been better.

Ruth Burgess

THE JOURNEY AHEAD

Bless O God,
the journey ahead.
Bless the travelling
and the arrival.
Bless those who welcome
and those who accept hospitality,
that Christ may come among us
in journeying and in stillness.

Kate McIlhagga

LIFE IS A JOURNEY HOME

We arise and go forth on the journey before us,
knowing that where Christ leads,
life is a journey home.
Therefore we travel in faith, in hope and in love.

In the name and in the blessing of God,
Father, Son and Holy Spirit. Amen.

Ian Cowie

The Pilgrim Road

NIGHT AS CLEAR AS DAY
a blessing based on Psalm 139

May God, to whom night is as clear as day,
guide your feet as you go.

May God, who is with you when you sit and when you stand,
encompass you with love and lead you by the hand.

May God, who knows your path and the places where you rest,
be with you in your waiting, be your good news for sharing,
and lead you in the way that is everlasting.

Jan Sutch Pickard

FRIENDS AND SAINTS AND ANGELS

Bless us God
with saints to tell us stories
with angels to surprise us
with friends along the way.

Bless us God
with strength and joy and courage
all the length and breadth
of our nights and days.

Ruth Burgess

LAUGHTER ON YOUR WAY

May God be with you
this day and every day.

The faithfulness of God
to keep you safe.
The friendship of Jesus
to bring laughter on your way.
The fragrance of the Holy Spirit
to be your refreshing.

May God be with you
this day and every day.

Blessings Workshop

BLESSED BE OUR FEET

Blessed be our feet
that feel the beat
at the heart of life
and move us on
in dancing prayer.

Joy Mead

LORD OF EVERY PILGRIM HEART

Lord of every pilgrim heart,
bless our journeys
on these roads
we never planned to take,
but
through your
surprising wisdom
discovered
we
were
on …

    Peter Millar

BETWEEN THE CRACKS

May you always notice
the dazzling, beautiful white flowers
growing up between the cracks
And may your road be
full of little resurrections.

    Neil Paynter

TIME ALONE

May you enjoy time alone:
beside the wide sea,
beneath the far stars,
in the sun's warm rays,
in the gentle rain.
And may God
who is in the spaces
bless your walking
on the good earth.

Joy Mead

A PILGRIM PEOPLE

God be with us on our journey
Jesus guide us in your love
Lord, gift us through each other
A pilgrim people renew.

da Noust

YOU WHO WALK WITH US

You who walk
with us
every step
of the way,
bless with
your presence
even
these strange contradictions
which are
on most days
markers in our lives.

Peter Millar

JOURNEY BLESSING

God be with you
on the road of life's suffering.
Christ be with you
in celebration.
The Spirit be with you
to encourage and bless you
at all times and in all time.

Kate McIlhagga

Responsive Blessings

THE BLESSING OF PEACE

Upon the family of God,

The blessing of God the Father of us all. **Amen.**

Upon you beloved sons, beloved daughters,

The Father's Blessing. **Amen.**

Upon your homes, families and work,

The Father's Blessing. **Amen.**

Between you all, old and young,

The Peace of the Lord Jesus.

Between those who have quarrelled,

The Peace of the Lord Jesus.

Between those with different understandings of the faith,

The Peace of the Lord Jesus.

Upon those who have confessed their sin and weakness,

The Peace of the Lord Jesus.

Upon those who have been hurt by the sin of others,

The Peace of the Lord Jesus.

Upon those who are ill in body or troubled in mind,

The Peace of the Lord Jesus.

To you who struggle with injustice and wrong,

The Peace of the Lord Jesus.

To you who bring healing of mind or of body to others,

The Peace of the Lord Jesus.

To you who seek to spread the good news of the love of God in Jesus,
The Peace of the Lord Jesus

To guide you in the way that you should go,
The Spirit of Peace in you.
To equip you to meet every challenge,
The Spirit of Peace in you.
To sanctify you through and through,
The Spirit of Peace in you.

The Peace that passes all human understanding be yours. **Amen.**
The Peace which the world cannot give be yours. **Amen.**
The Peace which Jesus gives be yours. **Amen.**

Be at Peace now

(silence)

In the name of the Father and of the Son and of the Holy Spirit. **Amen.**

Ian Cowie

An Evening Blessing

The sun has set over the hills of the western sky,
Lord, keep us in your gaze.
The evening's shadow falls across the moor,
Lord, keep us in your light.
The sky darkens and the stars fill the night,
Lord, keep us in your heart.
The tracks and paths are left behind,
Lord, keep us in your way.
Gracious God, Father, Son and Holy Spirit
bless and keep us and all your creatures
in your love this night.
Amen.

St Michael's (Princetown) Trust

Going onwards

As we prepare to leave this place and go onwards
to new discoveries and new challenges
let us ask for God's blessing.

May God bless us with the humility and humour
to be good travelling companions. **Amen.**

May God bless us with generosity
to those who experience dispossession and loss. **Amen.**

May God bless us with courage and creativity
in our journeying. **Amen.**

**In the name of God who takes the risk of creation,
of Jesus who journeyed to Calvary and beyond,
and the Spirit who kindles our hope and strength,
let us go in peace
and be witnesses of a renewed community of women and men
in the church. Amen.**

Frances Copsey

LIGHTER OF LIGHTS

Lighter of lights – **illumine us**
Fire of fires – **thaw us**
Power of powers – **strengthen us**
Lover of lovers – **warm us**

Teller of tales – **encourage us**
Destroyer of darkness – **save us**
Touchstone of truth – **examine us**
Summoner of stars – **amaze us**

Wellspring of wisdom – **weather us**
Water of life – **refresh us**
Dancer of days – **delight in us**
Breath of the universe – **bless us.**

Ruth Burgess

THE GLORY OF CHRIST IN CREATION BLESSING

O Christ whose glory shines through the stars:
fill our lives with your light
O Christ whose glory is seen in every plant and creature:
fill our lives with your love
O Christ whose glory fills the earth:
fill our lives with your power.

Bless us, teach us to live in peace with you and the earth and all its creatures, that your glory may continue to be witnessed among us. **Amen.**

St Michael's (Princetown) Trust

IN THE LOVE OF GOD

In the love of God
May we be warmed and welcomed

In the joy of Jesus
May we be strengthened and made whole

In the breath of the Spirit
May we be challenged and blessed.

Ruth Burgess

Autumn colour, harvest and mist

May the God who gives the Autumn colour,
enrich our lives with his presence.

May the God who gives the Autumn harvest,
sustain our lives with his love.

May the God who gives the Autumn mist,
enfold our lives with his peace.

May the God who in Jesus shows that life comes from death
bless us with his life,
now and for all eternity.
Amen.

St Michael's (Princetown) Trust

MAKER, STORYTELLER, BREATH OF LIFE

May God the maker bless us
May we grow wise and strong and holy

May God the storyteller bless us
May we know laughter and grace and healing

May God the breath of life bless us
May we be filled with courage and curiosity and joy

May God bless us now and always
May we travel homewards in love.

Ruth Burgess

A CLOSING BLESSING

A May the blessing of God surround us

B May angels and friends share our journey

A May we be safeguarded, loved and cherished

B May we walk on holy ground

A May people of faith inspire us

B May wisdom and justice empower us

A May we be wise and strong and creative

B May we celebrate life and hope

A May God's image grow within us

B May laughter and courage heal us

A May the Gospel of life sustain us

B All the days of our journey home.

Lines to be said responsively by two parts of the congregation (e.g. young and old, opposite sides of church, male and female ...).

Ruth Burgess

Blessings for Individuals

A BLESSING FOR AGNES MARY

May God bless you Agnes Mary:
May you be wise and strong and creative,
May you know the joy of Jesus,
May you dance in the wildness of the Spirit's breath.
May God's glory continue to grow in you,
gently, powerfully, tenderly.
May you be cradled in warmth and healing,
May you be held in God's wisdom and love.

Ruth Burgess

THE CANDLE I LIGHT

May the candle I light
be more than itself.
May it be for you:
the touch of a lover,
the smile of a child,
a drench of fresh rain,
a garden of sunflowers,
a good meal,

a dog to stroke,
a cup of clear water,
flowers for a friend,
a yes of breath,
a seed of hope,
a given moment …

May it be:
healing for your sickness;
closeness in your loneliness;
comfort in your mourning;
self-respect when you are rejected;
love to share.

May it be a moment
of shining in a tiny bit
of the darkness:
a hope,
a prayer,
a blessing.

          Joy Mead

A BLESSING FOR BRYAN

May God the starmaker
cradle you and circle you.
May God the storyteller
beckon and encourage you.
May God the life changer
challenge you and cherish you.

May you walk in
the light of God's love and laughter
all the moments of your nights and days.

Ruth Burgess

THE BLESSING OF JESUS – THE I AM

Jesus who is:

The Living Bread
feed you,
and give you strength to do his work,

The Light of the World
shine on you and
shine through you,

The Good Shepherd
guide you safely
through the green pastures
and through the dark valleys,

The Resurrection and Life
raise you up to
newness of life,

The Way, the Truth and the Life
lead you in His Way,
free you with His Truth,
heal you with His Life,

The True Vine
bear fruit through
your living
as you abide in Him.

The Alpha and the Omega
Be your be-all
your end-all,
your glory now
and through all eternity.

Ian Cowie

THE DARKNESS OF GOD: A BLESSING
(for John and Mike)

And the darkness of God will be to you a blessing
and the night shall become for you a path
And you shall walk in it with joy and gladness
and you shall run in it with head held high

And no marauding beast will assail you
and no unclean thing bar your way
For angels will guard you as you walk there
and guide you under the shadow of their wings

Until at last you reach the gate of hope
and go in under the doorway of delight
to be welcomed into the citadel of freedom
and to rest your soul under the portals of love

And there you shall be royally feasted
and seated in the banquet of love
And you shall hear your name called gently
and you shall enter into the darkness and gladness of God

And the blind shall lead you into God's dazzling darkness
and the deaf shall lead you into God's silent darkness
and the dumb shall lead you into God's eloquent darkness
and the lame shall lead you into God's dancing darkness

For in that city no lamp will shine
no sun or moon adorn the sky.
For the darkness of God will lighten every sadness
and the splendour of divine darkness will dazzle every eye.
And the fullness of divine glory will overshadow every longing
and the secret of divine beauty will satisfy every desire

And so the darkness of God shall be a blessing
and the shadow of God will be to you
a light more lovely than the dawn
a lamp more gleaming than the sun.
And your blindness shall be the mark of your faithfulness
and God's faithfulness shall be sealed by the star of everlasting night

This blessing was written for two friends – John Hull, who is blind, and Mike Holroyd, who is partially sighted. It deliberately attempts to use language and imagery from the experience of people with disabilities in a positive way.

-Nicola Slee

A mid-life birthday blessing for Frances

With the smile of God
may you be warmed and welcomed.

With the joy of Jesus
may you be circled and made whole.

With the breath of the Spirit
may you be challenged and safeguarded.

In the midst of your journey
may you meet God dancing
in night stars and angels
and snowdrops on frosty mornings.
May you be cherished,
may you be blessed.

Ruth Burgess

A blessing for one who is dying
(for Stuart)

As you have lived
in the light of truth
so may you die

As you have loved
in purity of heart
so may you be loved

As you have given
with generosity of hand
so may you now receive

As you have stood
in integrity of spirit
so may you now stand

As you have journeyed
with hopefulness of horizon
so may you still travel

As you have cared
with gentleness of touching
so may you now be held

And as you have radiated
the loving mercy of God
so may that loving mercy now guide, guard and protect you
into the final radiance.

Nicola Slee

A diamond wedding blessing for Joe and Eileen

A blessing Eileen,
a blessing on your living and loving;
a blessing from God your maker,
from Jesus your life giver,
from the Holy Spirit who fills you with wonder and joy.

A blessing from your friends past and present,
from the saints who have sat round your table,
from the angels who dance in and out of your days.

A blessing Joe,
a blessing on your loving and living;
a blessing from God your rock and sustainer,
from Jesus your storyteller,
from the Holy Spirit who fills you with wisdom and strength.

A blessing from the little ones you have nurtured and defended,
from the saints and the sinners you have cherished and befriended,
from the angels who have rejoiced in your boundaries
and guarded your stumps and bails.

A blessing Eileen and Joe
a blessing on your family
on the children you have cradled and let go into adulthood,
on the grandchild who carries your story on.

Sixty years is a long time for learning and loving and growing
and reflecting God's glory in the beauty of your lives.

A blessing on this house today and on your life together:
Joe and Eileen
may you continue to be
in love with God,
in love with life,
in love with each other.
And may God smile on you,
Jesus shelter you
and the Holy Spirit cherish you,
you and your children and your children's children,
all the hours and minutes
of your days and lives.

Ruth Burgess

A blessing for Mary on her 50th birthday

May the blessing of the Maker be yours
warmth and welcome and stars in the darkness
encircling you, hallowing you.

May the blessing of Jesus be yours
justice and adventure and bread for the journey
strengthening you, encouraging you.

May the blessing of the Holy Spirit be yours
wind and fire and a voice in the stillness
disturbing you, protecting you.

May the blessing of all God's children be yours
saints and friends and family and strangers
welcoming you, cherishing you.

Blessing and laughter and wisdom be yours Mary
May you be full of integrity and healing.
May you be strong and creative
and a teller of great stories.
May you party with the saints
and dance with the angels.
May you journey with God
all the length of your days.

Ruth Burgess

A BLESSING ON A NEW MEMBER OF THE IONA COMMUNITY

May the grace of God shine upon your face;

May the justice of God challenge you;

May the mercy of God encourage you;

May the courage of God support you in the dark times;

May the power of God keep you humble

and the humility of God inspire you;

May the generosity of God surprise you;

May the radiance of God dazzle you;

May the faithfulness of God give you hope – today and always.

Norman Shanks

A PRAYER FOR ALICE AND HER FAMILY

You are here
watching over me
giving me strength.

You are here
smiling with me,
dancing in and out
of the memories
of all my nights and days.

You are here
when the hours are long,
when I am weary
or worried
or in pain.

You are here
when I want to hang on
to the moments,
when I do not want
to let them go.

You are here,
and you hear me
when I ask you questions,
when I ask for help.

You are here with me.
You are with those I love.
I am glad you are looking after us.
Thank you.

Please bless and keep us
all the roads that we travel
on our journey home.

Ruth Burgess

THE PEOPLE GOD CALLS BLESSED

If I'm reading it right*
the people God calls blessed
are the ones who
feed the hungry
welcome the stranger
befriend those in trouble
care for those in pain.

Not a word about
who or what they do or don't believe in,
only a description of how they live their lives.

So I ask a blessing, God,
on my friends
who cannot
or do not
believe in you.
A blessing that they are not expecting
yet one which they will recognise.
A blessing of joy, integrity and justice,
a blessing of love and life.

                              Ruth Burgess

*Matthew 25 v 34–46

More Little Blessings

A WELCOMING BLESSING

May you meet God
in every place, in every person
and in the depths of your own heart.

Jan Sutch Pickard

GOD BLESS OUR GOOD DREAMING

God bless our good dreaming.
Lift us out of our dull and lifeless moments
so that we may tumble with fools,
skip with children,
walk on water
and fly with angels.

Joy Mead

MAY GOD HOLD YOU AS A LOVER

May God hold you as a lover,
May she caress your broken places,
May she dust you with gentleness,
And may you live in the world
As a sign of her touch.

Rosie Miles

THE BLESSING OF A TOY

God bless to you
this *doll* little one
May s(he) bring you joy.
God bless to you
this toy little one
May s(he) teach you tenderness
and encourage your imagination
to soar.

Kate McIlhagga

STRENGTH, PEACE AND WILDNESS

The strength of God for you.
The peace of the Son for you.
The wildness of the Spirit for you.
And may the Holy Three-in-One
protect and nurture you
on your journey.

Blessings Workshop

THE BLESSING OF SILENCE

(a prayer where the silences are as important as the words)

Listening God, we thank you for the blessing of silence.

Silence of sunrise.

Silence of mist on the hills.

Silence of listening.

Silence at the end of the story.

Silence between notes of music.

Silence between friends.

Amen.

Jan Sutch Pickard

BLESSING FOR LOVERS

May the God of all desire
kindle our loving and longing
that, through the yearning of our lives,
her justice and beauty may be revealed.

Nicola Slee

Blessing at the table

As the many threads are made one in the cloth,
as the many grains are made one in the bread,
as the many grapes are made one in the wine,
so we who are many are made one
as we stand around this table
laid with the one cloth
set with the one cup
fed with the one loaf.

Nicola Slee

CHRIST OF EVERY SUFFERING HEART

Christ of every suffering heart,
bless our awakening
as we begin to
discern more and more
your presence of life
within
the tortured
the abandoned
the persecuted
the imprisoned
the exploited
the betrayed
the violated
the abused
the silenced.

       Peter Millar

RUBBER BAND BLESSING

God give me the grace and space
to hold things together –
with a bit of bounce!

       Jan Sutch Pickard

The wonder of the ordinary

May you be wholly present
in your own life,
ready to be surprised
by the wonder of each ordinary
moment.

> Joy Mead

Dreams and visions

May the God of dreams and visions,
enable you to dream creatively
and to hear the dreaming of others –
young and old – in your community.
May you be open to new ideas,
dare to share visions,
be encouraged to hope.

> Jan Sutch Pickard

ALL AND EVERY ONE OF US

Bless us God.
All of us God.
Every one of us.
Every part of us.
We want to be full of your love and creativity.
We want to be full of You.

                              Ruth Burgess

BLESSING FOR A POET
(for Neil)

Your poem
is not simply about the words you choose
or even the words that choose you.
It is about being
the way you are –
sometimes without rhyme or reason
but always with integrity and passion.
May the Maker bless
all you are making of your life,
as you discover that of God in you.

                          Jan Sutch Pickard

A BLESSING FOR FRIDAY 13TH

For this day take no chances
Ring all the bells, burn
Incense everywhere, light
Dozens of candles,
Ask aid from the angels,
Yell praise to the saints

This is the superstition.
However, trust in God,
Enjoy the company of the 3 in 1 and

1 in
3, and you'll be held safely in mystery and in love.
the blessing of God be in you,
hope, laughter, healing and holy joy.

Ruth Burgess

GOD BLESS THE SNOW

God bless the snow
that wakens the
child in us,
beckoning us out
into a magic world
of sparkling beauty:
the gift of today.

Ruth Burgess

BLESSINGS FOR A MOTHER AND HER FAMILY

Bless you and your family as you face each day
Leaping the hurdles life throws in your way
Endurance, your strength, when you open your eyes
Smiles of love and warmth, easing their sighs
Sunshine is what you bring to their lives
Instilling security and strong family ties
Nurturing,
Growing strong, keeping trouble at bay
So bless you and your family as you face each day.

Angela Crossley

Bless and caress us

The light of God
to lead us.
The power of God
to hold us.
The joy of God
to heal us.
The grace of God
to bless us.
The love of God
to caress us.

Ruth Burgess

Writing Blessings
- some reflections and resources

WRITING BLESSINGS
– some reflections and resources

A good way to prepare to write blessings is to study some of the rich variety of blessings that can be found within religious traditions. My own inheritance, and that of most of the writers of this collection of blessings, is the Western Christian tradition, and for many of us a Celtic Christian tradition. Christianity, however, is not the only religion that embraces blessing prayers and actions, and a study of sacred writings from a wide range of faith traditions can add to an understanding and awareness of the blessing of God.

The most accessible source of blessings within Jewish writings is the Daily Prayer Book.[1] It includes blessing prayers within daily, Sabbath and festival worship as well as a collection of blessings for eating and drinking and enjoying the wonders of creation. More recent material includes work by rabbis Michael Shire[2] and Marcia Prager[3].

The Old and New Testaments of the Bible record a number of blessings. These include: Numbers 6 v 22–24; Romans 15 v 13; Philippians 3 v 7, 1; Thessalonians 5 v 23, 2; Thessalonians 3 v 16; Hebrews 13 v 20; and 2 John 1 v 3.

Within the Celtic tradition the most widely available collection is *Carmina Gadelica* collected by Alexander Carmichael in the highlands of Scotland between 1855 and 1910.[4] There are also many early examples available from Wales and Ireland: *God's Presence Makes the World*, A.M. Allchin[5] and *Celtic Christian Spirituality*, Oliver Davies and Fiona Bowie.[6]

Contemporary examples of blessings that draw on the Celtic tradition can be found in the writings of David Adam[7] and the liturgies of the Northumbrian

Community[8]. Many of the blessings found within the prayers and liturgies of the Iona Community also draw on the prayers and theology of the Celtic Church.[9]

For those wishing to explore the broader context of Celtic Christianity the writings of Ian Bradley provide a wide range of source material.[10] In *Celtic Christianity, Making Myths and Dreams*[11], he both describes and analyses the major movements of Celtic Christian revivalism in the British Isles.

Within Celtic material a wide range of adjectives and images are used to describe the nature and actions of God: e.g. *Lightener of the stars*[12], *King of the elements*[13], etc. Often the imagery reflects the social patterns of the writers' world: *Chief of chiefs*[14], *Herdsman of the flocks*[15]. The topics of the blessings acknowledge the presence of God in the details of daily life: fire making[16], caring for flocks[17], reaping the corn[18], getting up in the morning[19] and going to bed at night[20]. Many Celtic blessings have a Trinitarian structure[21] and often make reference to saints and angels, particularly to the protection of Michael and Bride[22].

One of the things that I have found useful in the process of writing blessings is to keep an alphabetical notebook of names that are given to God and to add to it as I discover new ones. I note down any phrases or images that capture my imagination and widen my picture of God's activity and nature. I also keep a list of verbs and adverbs which can be used to describe the actions of God.

When writing a blessing it is helpful to think about the type of blessing that you want to create. It could be a blessing of praise to God that you are writing for your own use. It may be a blessing that you have been asked to compose for someone else or for a particular occasion. If you are writing a blessing for someone else it may be helpful to recall what you know about the person and to try and use imagery that reflects their experience and will nurture their relationship with God. Similarly, if you are writing a blessing for an occasion, it is helpful to explore what you know about the occasion and who may be involved in it. If you are creating a blessing that will be used in public worship it might be appropriate to formulate a responsive blessing, which enables participants both to give and receive a blessing. You might want to suggest an action to accompany the blessing.

If you are writing a blessing that will be read out loud it is important to read it out loud yourself, and to ask yourself or a listener: *How does it sound? Is the rhythm steady? Do the sounds the blessing makes give a feeling of what I am trying to say? Might other words sound better?*

When I am writing a blessing I often ask myself questions as I am writing. *What does it feel like for me to be blessed by God? How does God want me to feel? What might God want to give the person for whom I am writing this blessing?* I might think about the person or the situation. I might be silent for a few moments and then try and find words to express the pictures that come into my mind. Sometimes I scribble a list of words down the margin of an unfinished blessing and read them out loud to see if one of them sounds better than the others. Sometimes I write down a list of ideas and images and work from there.

The layout and punctuation of blessings tends, as in poetry, to be executed according to the writer's preference! If you work on a computer you may find that each line will be given an initial capital letter and you might want to amend this. Punctuation and layout within the context of a blessing is a means of telling the reader what to emphasise and where to pause. Reading the blessing out loud should guide you as to what punctuation is necessary.

When writing a blessing that will be printed on a service paper or read out loud, the inclusion of an *Amen* (so be it), enables the congregation to give vocal assent to the prayer. If the blessing is for individual use an *Amen* is sometimes included but often not.

Writing a prayer of blessing demands, among other things, a discipline similar to that of writing poetry. Within Celtic culture the role of a poet included the declaring of the goodness of God and the discernment of God's presence in all created things. Both priests and poets were called upon to praise and bless. As in writing poetry sometimes the words of a blessing come easily; at other times the words and ideas come slowly and require much re-working.

As noted in the introduction there is a biblical tradition that those who pray prayers of blessing for others will themselves be blessed. My experience is that those who write prayers of blessing for others frequently find themselves caught up in the joy and blessing of God.

REFERENCES

1. Singer, S., *The Authorised Daily Prayer Book of the United Hebrew Congregations*. 1st edition 1890. Centenary edition 1990. Revised 1998.
2. Shire, M., Rabbi Dr, *L'Chaim: Prayers and Blessings for the Home*. Frances Lincoln Ltd, 2000.*
3. Prager, M., Rabbi, *The Path of Blessing*. Bell Tower, New York, 1998.*
4. Carmichael, A., *Carmina Gadelica*. Floris Books, 1992.
5. Allchin, A.M., *God's Presence Makes the World*. Darton, Longman and Todd Ltd, 1997.
6. Davies, O. and Bowie, F., *Celtic Christian Spirituality*. SPCK, 1997.
7. Adam, D., *The Edge of Glory: Prayers in the Celtic Tradition*. Triangle/SPCK, 1985.
8. *Celtic Daily Prayer from the Northumbrian Community*. Harper Collins, 2000.

9. Wild Goose Worship Group, *A Wee Worship Book*. Wild Goose Publications with the Wild Goose Worship Group, 1999.

    The Iona Community, *Iona Abbey Worship Book*. Wild Goose Publications, 2001.

    Galloway, K. (ed), *The Pattern of Our Days: Liturgies and Resources for Worship*. Wild Goose Publications, 2001.

    Burgess, R. and Galloway, K. (eds), *Praying For the Dawn: A Resource Book for the Ministry of Healing*. Wild Goose Publications, 2000.

10. Bradley, I., *The Celtic Way*. Darton, Longman and Todd Ltd, 1993.

    Bradley, I., *Columba: Pilgrim and Penitent*. Wild Goose Publications, 1996.

11. Bradley, I., *Celtic Christianity: Making Myths and Chasing Dreams*. 1999, Edinburgh University Press.

12. Carmichael, A., Op.cit. No 16.

13. Ibid. No.119.

14. Ibid. No.334.

15. Ibid. No. 97.

16. Ibid. No. 82.

17. Ibid. No. 104.

18. Ibid. No. 89.

19. Ibid. No. 226.

20. Ibid. No. 26.

21. Ibid. Nos. 249, 32, 277.

22. Ibid. No. 339.

NOTES:

Those books marked with a * can be obtained via: The Progressive Jewish Bookshop, 80 East End Road, London N3 2SY. Phone 0208 349 9484.

Running a Blessings Workshop

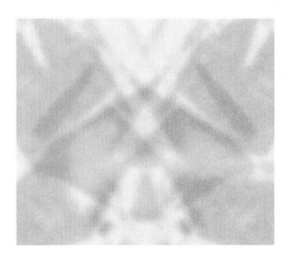

Running a blessings workshop

A number of blessings in this collection come from blessings workshops that have been run either as part of a day of liturgy workshops or as an independent activity. I have found that 10/12 people are the optimum number for running a workshop and that 70/90 minutes is about the right length of time. Some groups may take a little longer depending on how much discussion takes place.

If it is possible to have contact with workshop members before the workshop, it can be productive to ask people to bring their favourite blessing with them to the workshop and to be willing to share with the group the reasons they chose to bring it. This is also a good way for the workshop leader to add to their collection of blessings!

If you have access to a photocopier during the workshop it should be possible for all group members to be given copies of the blessings brought to and written during the workshop. Alternatively these can be photocopied and distributed after the event.

You will need to provide pens and paper for this workshop. Also crayons or felt-tips and pieces of card, around postcard size, and a box or basket to receive and distribute the cards. If you have more than one room at your disposal, some people may appreciate a quiet corner in which to think and write (make sure that you give them a time to come back to the group).

- Introduce yourself to the group and explain the process of the workshop. Allow the group to introduce themselves to each other.

- Look at some dictionary definitions of BLESS and BLESSING.

- Look at some examples of blessings: from the Bible, from the traditions of the group, *Carmina Gadelica*[1] or any other sources that you think appropriate. Read some of them out loud around the group.

- If participants have brought blessings with them, invite them to share them with the group.

- Spend some time looking at the structure of a number of blessings – at rhythms and patterns – images of God – beginnings and endings, etc. Talk about the actions that sometimes accompany blessings.

- Provide pens and paper and invite the group to write a blessing for an individual, but not specifically for an individual member of the group. Also provide crayons and cards and ask participants to copy their blessing onto a card and illustrate it (a simple drawing or pattern) and then to place it in a central box or basket. As well as the illustrated blessing card ask participants to make a small copy of their blessing and give it to you in order that you can photocopy all the blessings and later distribute them to group members. This activity should take around 20 minutes. **NB** I usually have some books of blessings in the room and suggest to people that if they cannot think of anything to write they could choose and copy a blessing from a book and illustrate it. I have found, in practice, that people rarely need to do this, but it does provide a safety-net for those who find it difficult to begin to write.

- When everyone has finished their blessing card, and given you a copy of it, bring the group back together. Divide the group into pairs (if your group had an uneven number of participants you will have needed to write a blessing yourself). Hand the basket/box round the room and ask people to pick out a

164

blessing for their partner. If their partner spots that they are about to receive their own blessing an exchange is made.

- When everyone has picked out a blessing for their partner, suggest to the group that they go away in pairs, find somewhere suitable and read their partner's blessing to them and give them their blessing card to keep.

- If the group has another activity to take part in you will need to specify a time and place to come back together.

The workshop I have described is focused on writing personal blessings but the format could also be adapted for writing other types of blessings – seasonal blessings, journey blessings, etc.

BLESSINGS WORKSHOP – SUGGESTED TIMESCALE	
ACTIVITIES	MINUTES
INTRODUCTIONS AND PROCESS	10–15
DICTIONARY DEFINITIONS	5
VARIOUS EXAMPLES	10–15
PARTICIPANTS' EXAMPLES	10–15
STRUCTURE OF BLESSINGS	10
WRITING AND ILLUSTRATING	20–25
DISTRIBUTING BLESSINGS	5
READING BLESSING TO PARTNER	5
TOTAL	75–95

REFERENCES

1 Carmichael, A., Op.cit.

INDEX OF AUTHORS (with page numbers)

NOTES:

a   The prayer credited to Anon was originally titled 'Medicine' and was first published in *The Big Issue in Scotland*, City Lights section, Issue 296 (October 26–November 1, 2000).

b   The prayers credited to Blessings Workshops were written during workshops run by the editor and were not signed by the participants. If you have attended a workshop and recognise your own work, please write and let me know and it will be acknowleged in the next edition. My apologies that I was not able to credit it specifically in this edition.

c   This blessing was written by Jenni Fuchs inspired by prayers written by the children of St Columba's by the Castle Junior Church, Edinburgh.

d   St Michael's (Princetown) Trust promotes care and concern for the environment and takes inspiration from its Dartmoor location. Prayers from the trust are copyright and are used with permission.

e   *da* Noust is an informal circle of members and friends of L'Arche, Edinburgh. L'Arche is an ecumenical community welcoming adults with learning difficulties, assistants and others to a shared life. The word Noust is Orcadian for a boat shelter on the shore, a place to withdraw for rest and renewal, prior to setting out fishing once more in the morning.

Many traditional hymnbooks have musical settings to blessings, particularly the Aaronic blessing – *The Lord bless you and keep you.*.

Also available are:
Aaronic blessing   LFB
Bless the Lord my soul   CG
Now go in peace   CG
O Bless the Lord   CAYP
The peace of the earth   CG
Wen Ti – May the Lord, mighty God   SBTL
(Wen Ti is a Chinese setting used for occasions when a congregation wishes to ask a blessing for an individual.)

CAYP   *Come All You People: Shorter Songs for Worship*, by John Bell
LFB   *Love From Below* (Wild Goose Songs, vol. 3)
SBTL   *Sent by the Lord: Songs of the World Church*, Volume 2, edited and arranged by John Bell
All published by Wild Goose Publications, Glasgow.

CG   *Common Ground: A Song Book for All the Churches* (Saint Andrew Press, 1998, Edinburgh)

Oran, an ecumenical partnership of musicians, have composed some musical settings to prayers from *Carmina Gadelica*. They can be contacted at 38 Glenfarg Road, Catford, London SE6 1XH. Website at http:members.aol.com/OranMusic

Many of the blessings by *da* Noust have musical settings which are available from *da* Noust, 132 Constitution Street, Edinburgh EH6 6AJ.

THE IONA COMMUNITY

The Iona Community, founded in 1938 by the Revd George MacLeod, then a parish minister in Glasgow, is an ecumenical Christian community committed to seeking new ways of living the Gospel in today's world. Initially working to restore part of the medieval abbey on Iona, the Community today remains committed to 'rebuilding the common life' through working for social and political change, striving for the renewal of the church with an ecumenical emphasis, and exploring new, more inclusive approaches to worship, all based on an integrated understanding of spirituality.

The Community now has over 240 Members, about 1500 Associate Members and around 1500 Friends. The Members – women and men from many denominations and backgrounds (lay and ordained), living throughout Britain with a few overseas – are committed to a fivefold Rule of devotional discipline, sharing and accounting for use of time and money, regular meeting, and action for justice and peace.

At the Community's three residential centres – the Abbey and the MacLeod Centre on Iona, and Camas Adventure Camp on the Ross of Mull – guests are welcomed from March to October and over Christmas. Hospitality is provided for over 110 people, along with a unique opportunity, usually through week-long programmes, to extend horizons and forge relationships through sharing an experience of the common life in worship, work, discussion and relaxation. The Community's shop on Iona, just outside the Abbey grounds, carries an attractive range of books and craft goods.

The Community's administrative headquarters are in Glasgow, which also serves as a base for its work with young people, the Wild Goose Resource Group working in the field of worship, a bi-monthly magazine, *Coracle*, and a publishing house, Wild Goose Publications.

For information on the Iona Community contact:
The Iona Community
4th Floor, Savoy House,
140 Sauchiehall Street, Glasgow G2 3DH, UK
Phone: 0141 332 6393
e-mail: ionacomm@gla.iona.org.uk   web: www.iona.org.uk

For enquiries about visiting Iona, please contact:
Iona Abbey
Isle of Iona
Argyll PA76 6SN, UK
Phone: 01681 700404   e-mail: ionacomm@iona.org.uk

For book/tape/CD catalogues, contact:
Wild Goose Publications
4th Floor, Savoy House, 140 Sauchiehall Street,
Glasgow G2 3DH, UK
e-mail: admin@ionabooks.com
or see our products online at www.ionabooks.com

Praying for the Dawn

A resource book for the ministry of healing

Ruth Burgess and Kathy Galloway (eds)

A compilation of material from several writers with a strong emphasis on liturgies and resources for healing services. Many aspects of healing are addressed and the book includes a section of worship resources – prayers, responses, litanies, poems, meditations and blessings.

192pp · 1 901557 26 X · £10.99

Advent Readings from Iona

Brian Woodcock & Jan Sutch Pickard

Celebrate Christmas with reflections and prayers for each day of Advent. This effective antidote to the commercialism of the festive season can be used for individual meditation or group worship.

96pp · 1 901557 33 2 · £7.99

The One Loaf

An everyday celebration

Joy Mead

An illustrated book of stories, recipes, poems and prayers which explores the making and the mystery of bread – its growing, making and baking, and the holiness of eating and the justice of sharing.

160pp · 1 901557 38 3 · £10.99

Maker's Blessing

Prayers and meditations from the Iona Community

A pocket-sized, hardcover gift book of inspirational meditations and prayers.

48pp · 1 901557 24 3 · £4.99

The Iona Abbey Worship Book

The Iona Community

Services and resources used daily in the Abbey on the island of Iona reflecting the Iona Community's commitment to the belief that worship is all that we are and all that we do, with no division into the 'sacred' and the 'secular'. The material draws on many traditions, including the Celtic.

272pp · 1 901557 50 2 · £9.99

My Dinner With Anton

A book about St Seraphim of Sarov

Paul Wallis

An extraordinary over-dinner conversation between a 19th-century Russian Orthodox monk and a contemporary minister about the life and example of an intriguing Russian saint, Seraphim of Sarov, and the relevance of his teaching to modern western spirituality.

128pp · 1 901557 31 6 · £8.99

...ship including the work of the Wild Goose Resource Group... ...on meditation and reflection

If you would like to find out more about our books, tapes and CDs, contact us at:

Wild Goose Publications
Unit 16
Six Harmony Row
Glasgow G51 3BA
UK

Tel: +44 (0)141 440 0985
Fax: +44 (0)141 440 ...
e-mail: admin@ionabooks.com
...
or visit our website at...